CANADA IN THE GLOBAL AGE

Rennay Craats

Weigl

CALGARY

www.weigl.com

We acknowledge the financial support of the Government of Canada through the Book Publishing Industry Development Program (BPIDP) for our publishing activities.

Published by Weigl Educational Publishers Limited
6325 – 10 Street SE
Calgary, Alberta, Canada
T2H 2Z9

Web site: www.weigl.com

National Library of Canada Cataloguing-in-Publication Data

Craats, Rennay, 1973-
  Canada in the global age / Rennay Craats.

  Includes bibliographical references and index.
  ISBN 1-55388-017-X

  1. Canada--History--20th century. I. Title.
FC600.C72 2003   971.06   C2003-910136-3
F1034.2.C72 2003

Printed in the United States of America
1 2 3 4 5 6 7 8 9 0   07 06 05 04 03

Project Coordinator
Heather C. Hudak
Editor
Donald Wells
Photo Researcher
Wendy Cosh
Pamela Wilton
Designer
Warren Clark
Layout
Bryan Pezzi
Katherine Phillips

CONTENTS

Canada as a MIDDLE POWER

While Europe was devastated by World War II, Canada emerged largely unscathed.

Canada supported the Allied forces during World War II, 1939–1945. Volunteers signed up to fight overseas. Later, **mandatory** military service added more troops to the Allied effort. Canadian factories produced war goods such as ammunition, weapons, and clothing for soldiers. To further assist the war effort, Canadian citizens began to ration. They reduced their coffee, gasoline, meat, and sugar consumption. They also bought war bonds. Hundreds of thousands of women rushed to factories and workplaces to fill jobs left open by men who went off to fight. Others joined the military to perform nursing or clerical duties. During the war, Canada's reliance on Great Britain lessened. The common experiences and interests Canada shared with the United States became apparent. Canada and the U.S. became closer economic and military partners. They fought side by side to defeat the Axis Powers in 1945.

Once the war ended, Canada, along with China, Great Britain, the Soviet Union, and the U.S., signed peace treaties. Troops returned home heroes, and families were reunited. There was a large increase in the birth rate immediately after World War II. This "baby boom" along with increased **immigration**—mainly from Europe—increased Canada's population by 50 percent between 1941 and 1961. Many of these new families chose to live away from inner cities. More people owned automobiles in the 1940s, which made it possible for them to live farther from their workplace and public transportation systems. Wages were also rising, and many Canadians spent their extra income on larger homes. This freedom and **prosperity** gave rise to suburban areas.

FURTHER UNDERSTANDING

Cold War The Cold War between the United States and the Soviet Union lasted from 1945 to 1990. Although there was never any physical fighting, a war still occurred. In this case, the war was fought with words. The two most powerful nations, the U.S. and the Soviet Union, argued about which type of government and society was the best. The U.S. has always been a **democracy**, with a strong capitalist base. A **capitalist system** is based on the belief that private citizens have the right to own businesses and earn money on their own merit. The Soviet Union was a communist society. A **communist system** is based on the idea that the government controls all factories and production. The government then distributes the wealth evenly among its citizens so that poverty is eliminated.

War bonds During World War II, Canadian citizens who invested money in the war effort were issued war bonds by the government. After the war, the government created Canada Savings Bonds to encourage citizens to continue saving.

■ Victory in Europe came on May 8, 1945. Many celebrations took place, such as a VE-Day parade on Sparks Street in Ottawa, Ontario.

Canada had proven itself a power independent of Great Britain, earning it designation as a "middle power." This meant that Canada's influence was recognized, but it was still too small to dominate international affairs. Canada was the fourth-largest Allied power, and its location made it ideal for both Atlantic and Pacific trade areas. Since Canada is located between the Soviet Union and the U.S., as tensions between the two countries grew, Canada was literally stuck in the middle. Either country could use the route over Canada to attack the other. These tensions, known as the Cold War, grew throughout the 1950s and 1960s, bringing the world to the brink of another world war.

While Europe was devastated by World War II, Canada emerged largely unscathed. Canadian industry was intact, and had expanded to meet wartime demands. Hard times created by the Great Depression of the 1930s were over. The post-war economy was strong, and the country was prosperous. Unemployment was no longer a problem, and the booming economy created competition for workers. The discovery of oil in the West further boosted the economy in the 1940s. **Inflation** was controlled, and the standard of living rose.

The war also created a larger government in the country. After the war, government at all levels continued to grow, and Canada introduced social welfare programs. Unemployment Insurance was introduced, and Children's Allowance, also known as the "baby bonus," provided families with children monthly payments for food and clothing.

Life in Canada was very different after World War II. The threat of nuclear war changed the way people thought and lived. The two superpowers after the war, the Soviet Union and the U.S., divided the world into two camps. Although World War II was fought overseas, it brought about changes that swept across Canada and the world. The experiences of the 1940s led to a new time for the country. Canada had entered the Global Age.

■ Canada's booming economy in the 1940s and 1950s allowed homeowners to purchase more items for their homes, including television sets.

Voices of DISCONTENT

In 1973, the Supreme Court of Canada ruled that Native Peoples' rights did exist.

Feminism

During World War II, women accepted new roles in society. Women who had been homemakers were now making guns as they filled factory jobs once held by men. Women also drove taxicabs, built ships, made ammunition, and packed meat. By 1944, nearly 1 million women had entered the work force. Many working women wore their hair short or wrapped in a scarf to prevent it from becoming tangled in machinery. Women also began wearing pants instead of skirts and dresses. When the war ended, women were expected to return to their traditional roles and jobs.

In the 1960s and 1970s, women began advocating for economic, political, and social equality. Through public demonstrations, the women's liberation movement demanded reforms. Women started wearing blue jeans, T-shirts, and flat shoes. They challenged society to take another look at the role of women.

As a result of women's liberation, more women sought jobs outside the home during the 1960s. By 1971, more than 30 percent of married women were employed in the work force. Ten years later, that number increased to nearly 50 percent. By 2000, the number of married women in the workplace was 70 percent. Reforms brought about by women's liberation included working after marriage, keeping one's maiden name after marriage, and being called "Ms." rather than "Miss" or "Mrs."

Peace Protests

During the 1960s, fear of nuclear war spread across Canada. The army acquired missiles that could be armed with nuclear **warheads**. The government signed defence agreements with the United States and the North Atlantic Treaty Organization (NATO). Political opposition parties, social groups, and students protested against nuclear warheads, or "nukes,"

FURTHER UNDERSTANDING

Women's liberation
Women's liberation was a push for equality in a society dominated by men. "Women's libbers" demanded changes to roles in society—from equality in the workplace to family rooms in public restrooms.

Women's work Women's work was considered homemaking, nursing, teaching, and secretarial positions. After the war, government and private companies gave jobs that were being performed by women back to returning soldiers. Some women fought to keep their jobs, but many others returned to their traditional lives.

■ The exclusive, male-only Rideau Club in Ottawa was the site of a women's liberation protest lunch in 1972. Today, 148 of the club's 900 members are women.

and Canadian involvement in nuclear weapons testing.

Many people called for a ban on nuclear weapons testing, but the practice continued. In 1999, the British Columbia and Canadian governments negotiated for the continued use of Nanoose Bay, British Columbia, for American nuclear weapons testing. The province did not want nuclear weapons testing. The federal government took over the area to allow for continued testing. Thousands of Canadians wrote to the federal government and made presentations against the takeover and weapons testing. Despite these challenges, the federal government took ownership of the area and offered the United States a 10-year extension of their 1965 agreement. This allowed the U.S. Navy to continue using the Nanoose Bay testing range. Many Canadians continued **lobbying** for change.

Native Peoples Rise Up

In the 1970s, **activism** extended to the Aboriginal community, causing disputes over land claims to escalate. In many places, no formal treaties were signed between the

government and Aboriginal groups. Many Aboriginal groups argued that they had never given up their rights to the land. The Nisga'a peoples of northern British Columbia had been fighting for the title to their land since the 1890s. Throughout history, the government had overlooked Native Peoples' claims. In 1973, the Supreme Court of Canada ruled that Aboriginal rights did exist, and provincial governments began negotiating land-claim settlements.

In the 1970s, some Aboriginal leaders called for **amendments** to Canada's Indian Act. Changes were made to the Indian Act in 1985. When the Canadian **Constitution** was being rewritten, many Native Peoples demanded that it include Aboriginal rights and self-government. For weeks, Aboriginal groups lobbied the government until their rights were included in the new constitution. Disputes over Aboriginal rights and affairs were not resolved with the constitution. Discontent and protests continued through the 1980s, 1990s, and into the twenty-first century.

■ On April 13, 2000, the Canadian government passed the Nisga'a Treaty. The treaty provides the Nisga'a peoples with the right to self-government. Chief Rod Robinson is the Nisga'a ambassador.

Early Political LEADERS

W. L. Mackenzie King (1875–1950)

W. L. Mackenzie King was elected prime minister four times between 1921 and 1945. In 1939, his loyalty was divided between Great Britain and his desire to keep Canada from taking part in World War II. King supported the war effort and mediated relations between the United States and Great Britain.

In 1942, the majority of Canadians—with the exception of Quebec—favoured conscription, or mandatory military service. In 1944, heavy losses of Canadian soldiers made it necessary for King to institute conscription. The war ended in 1945. Few of the conscripted soldiers arrived in Europe in time to fight.

In 1945, Prime Minister King was reelected with another majority government. He continued to represent Canada at international conferences. In 1947, he chose Louis St. Laurent to finish his term as prime minister. King resigned in 1948.

Louis St. Laurent (1882–1973)

Louis St. Laurent was respected by both French and English Canadians. During his time as prime minister, Canada experienced industrial growth and a booming economy. St. Laurent involved Canada in global politics by supporting the United Nations and the North Atlantic Treaty Organization (NATO). He invited Newfoundland to join Confederation in 1949 and worked to improve relations between French and English Canada.

After St. Laurent's second election, his health declined and economic, political, and administrative conflicts emerged. During the 1957 election, Conservative John G. Diefenbaker won with a large majority of seats. Soon after, St. Laurent retired from politics.

FURTHER UNDERSTANDING

Confederation On July 1, 1867, Ontario, Quebec, New Brunswick, and Nova Scotia became the Dominion of Canada. Though Canada remained part of the British Empire, it now had independent governing authority. The remaining six provinces and three territories joined later. Sir John A. Macdonald was elected the first prime minister of Canada.

North Atlantic Treaty Organization (NATO) NATO is a defence alliance created in 1949 by Belgium, Canada, Denmark, France, Great Britain, Iceland, Italy, Luxembourg, the Netherlands, Norway, Portugal, and the United States. It was established to strengthen the stability, well-being, and freedom of its members through collective security.

United Nations (UN) The UN is an international organization of 191 countries. It was established in 1945 to promote world co-operation and peace by developing strong relationships between countries, using co-operation to resolve conflicts, and promoting respect for human rights.

■ William Lyon Mackenzie King served as prime minister for 22 years—longer than any other Canadian prime minister.

John G. Diefenbaker (1895–1979)

John G. Diefenbaker became prime minister after the Liberals resigned from office in 1957. In 1958, Diefenbaker was elected with the largest majority government in Canadian history. He introduced the Bill of Rights in 1960. This **legislation** protects people's basic rights, such as the freedom of speech and the freedom to practise one's religion. Diefenbaker also tried to improve human rights in other countries, such as South Africa.

Diefenbaker worked to improve relations with Canada's Native Peoples. He gave them the right to vote in federal elections and the right to own property.

He appointed the first Aboriginal senator, James Gladstone.

In 1959, Diefenbaker cancelled the Avro Arrow project, an initiative to build fighter planes. As a result, 14,000 Canadians lost their jobs. In 1962, Diefenbaker was reelected with a minority government. In 1963, he had to call another election after receiving a vote of non-confidence. Diefenbaker lost the election to Liberal Lester B. Pearson, but continued to serve as the opposition leader until 1967. He was a Member of Parliament until his death in 1979.

Lester B. Pearson (1897–1972)

Lester B. Pearson proved his leadership skills during the Suez Canal Crisis in 1956. He recommended that a peacekeeping force enter the area and supervise the withdrawal of troops. The UN agreed, and Canadians led the peacekeeping team. This action earned Pearson the Nobel Peace Prize in 1957. He also won the Liberal Party leadership and was elected prime minister in 1963.

Pearson created the Royal Commission on Bilingualism and Biculturalism. The Royal Commission made federal services available in both French and English. For more than 1 year, Pearson fought for a distinctly Canadian flag—the Maple Leaf flew for the first time in 1965. He also established the Canada Pension Plan. In 1968, 71-year-old Pearson retired from politics.

■ In 1957, Lester B. Pearson became the first Canadian to receive a Nobel Prize. He was awarded the prize for his efforts to bring peace to regions where conflict existed.

Recent Political LEADERS

Pierre Trudeau became a celebrity before he was elected prime minister.

Pierre Trudeau (1919–2000)

Pierre Trudeau became a celebrity before he was elected prime minister in 1968. During "Trudeaumania," as many as 16,000 people attended rallies for him.

Trudeau passed the Official Languages Act in 1969, making both French and English Canada's official languages. In 1970, the *Front de Libération du Québec* (FLQ) used violence to express their **separatist** ideals during the October Crisis. Trudeau invoked the War Measures Act.

Trudeau won the 1972 election with a minority government, but he won a majority government during the 1974 election. He battled inflation and tried to create jobs. In 1979, Trudeau lost the election to Conservative Joe Clark. Eight months later, members of Parliament passed a vote of non-confidence in Clark's leadership, and another election was called. Trudeau agreed to return as Liberal leader and won the 1980 election.

Trudeau introduced the Constitution Act and the Charter of Rights and Freedoms in 1982. Trudeau resigned from office in 1984.

Joe Clark (1939–)

Joe Clark was elected prime minister in May 1979. At age 39, he was Canada's youngest prime minister. During his campaign, Clark promised to cut taxes and increase economic growth. Once in office, he proposed tax increases and decreased economic growth. Clark resigned when his proposed tax hikes were defeated.

FURTHER UNDERSTANDING

The Constitution and the Charter of Rights and Freedoms In 1982, Great Britain gave Canada its constitution. The Constitution of Canada is a set of rules used to govern the nation. The Charter of Rights and Freedoms was added to ensure all Canadian citizens receive fair treatment under the government.

Free trade Free trade between Canada, the U.S., and Mexico involved the gradual removal of tariffs and other barriers restricting the trade of items produced in North America. In 1994, the three countries signed the North American Free Trade Agreement (NAFTA)—creating a free trade zone.

War Measures Act The War Measures Act is a legislated suspension of rights, allowing police to arrest and hold suspects without following the usual rule of law.

Vote of non-confidence When members of parliament lose confidence in the prime minister's ability to lead the country, an election is called. Prime Minister Joe Clark was forced to call an election after only 7 months in office.

■ Trudeaumania swept across Canada during the 1968 federal election. Pierre Trudeau signed autographs for the crowds of people who gathered to meet him.

John Turner (1929–)

John Turner assumed the role of prime minister when Trudeau retired in 1984. He held office for less than 4 months before losing the federal election to Brian Mulroney. Turner resigned as the Liberal Party leader in 1990.

Brian Mulroney (1939–)

Brian Mulroney was elected prime minister in 1984. In 1987, he announced a plan for a free trade agreement with the United States. In 1990, Mexico joined the agreement to form the North American Free Trade Agreement (NAFTA). By 1994, the three countries had signed NAFTA, making continental free trade official.

Mulroney drafted the Meech Lake Accord in 1987 to recognize Quebec as a "distinct society" with special constitutional rights. The agreement was not passed. In 1992, Mulroney created the Charlottetown Accord. His second attempt to unite the country was not successful. At the same time, Mulroney's popularity had declined as a result of the Goods and Services Tax (GST), and free trade's failure to deliver prosperity and jobs. In 1993, Mulroney resigned as prime minister.

Avril (Kim) Campbell (1947–)

In 1993, Kim Campbell became Canada's first female prime minister. Campbell was elected leader of the Conservative Party after Mulroney announced his retirement in 1993. She held office for about 4 months before the Conservatives were defeated by the Liberals in the national election.

Jean Chrétien (1934–)

After spending decades involved in Liberal politics, Jean Chrétien became prime minister in 1993. In 1995, Quebeckers held a vote on their future—whether or not to separate from Canada. Canadians from coast to coast rallied to show their support for a Canada that included Quebec. The vote was very close, with only 50.6 percent of Quebeckers voting to stay in Canada. Although Chrétien was criticized for not doing enough to ensure Quebec stayed part of Canada, he was elected for a second term in 1997 with a majority government. He was elected again in 2000 with his third consecutive majority government.

■ Jean Chrétien has served with six prime ministers and held twelve ministerial positions. He was first elected to the House of Commons in 1963 as the Member of Parliament for Saint-Maurice-Lafleche, Quebec.

Cultural Communities in QUEBEC

Many Quebeckers realized they no longer shared Duplessis' ideals.

Quebec's relationship with the rest of Canada was unstable during the second half of the twentieth century. From 1936 to 1939, and 1944 to 1959, Union Nationale Party leader Maurice Duplessis was premier of Quebec. Duplessis worked to preserve the French-Canadian way of life by preventing English Canada's involvement in Quebec's provincial affairs. He rejected federal programs that influenced French life, hoping it would guarantee *la survivance*.

Duplessis refused English influence in **culture** and politics but invited it into Quebec's economy by offering industries **incentives** to operate in Quebec. People left Quebec's rural communities to work in the new industries.

In the 1940s and 1950s, Quebec witnessed labour unrest when workers rebelled against low pay and long hours. The government sided with industry, further enraging Quebec workers. In 1949, asbestos workers went on strike, gaining the support of Roman Catholic clergy, students, and intellectuals.

Duplessis ordered police to break the picket lines and arrest the leaders. Many Quebeckers realized they no longer shared Duplessis' ideals.

In 1959, Duplessis died and Jean Lesage's Liberals won a narrow victory over the Union Nationale. Lesage made many changes during his first few years as premier. This period was known as the Quiet Revolution. This social revolution saw an updated education system, the growth of labour unions, and a revamped social welfare system. The Liberal Party was now made up of journalists, lawyers, professors, and students. These educated groups aimed to protect and expand Quebec's interests in Canada. During the Quiet Revolution, Quebec's educational, cultural, and political level became more consistent with the rest of Canada.

■ During his term, Maurice Duplessis was responsible for adopting many symbols, such as the Quebec flag.

FURTHER UNDERSTANDING

La survivance La survivance was the survival of the French language and traditions. This was achieved by retaining the French language and the Roman Catholic faith, maintaining the traditions and values of rural life in the province, and encouraging obedience to authority, especially church leaders. Many Quebeckers wanted life in the province to be as it had been in the past—isolated from the rest of the country and from the postwar changes sweeping Canada.

Nationalist To be a nationalist is to have a strong devotion and pride in one's country. It is an extreme sense of patriotism.

Special status Jean Lesage believed that Quebec needed more powers than other provinces so it could protect its distinct language and culture. He wanted to opt out of many federal programs and have funding to create provincial programs for Quebeckers. He warned the federal government that it had to encourage Quebec to remain part of Canada or Confederation would collapse.

The Quiet Revolution created strong nationalist feelings in Quebec. The Quebec government's election slogan was *Maître chez nous,* which means "master in our own house." Though Jean Lesage was not seeking independence, he was demanding more control over Quebec. He wanted Quebec businesses to speak French, and he wanted to modernize Quebec's industries.

Many Quebeckers saw Canada as an unequal partnership between two nations—French and English. Lesage lobbied the federal government for special status for the province. He wanted recognition of the French language and culture. He also believed Quebec should have control over its own affairs. Prime Minister Pearson considered Lesage's concerns. Through the Bilingualism and Biculturalism Commission, Pearson hoped to find a balance between French and English Canada. The commission was the predecessor to Trudeau's Official Languages Act, in which French was recognized as an official language in Canada.

Lesage's government believed the act should extend beyond Quebec to other Canadian provinces. He called for equality for French-speaking minorities throughout Canada. He also set up a diplomatic outpost in Paris. The Quiet Revolution lasted 7 years, and it ended with a Liberal defeat at the election polls. Daniel Johnson and the Union Nationale regained power briefly with election success in 1966.

Before 1960, people in Quebec called themselves Canadiens. During the 1960s, they began describing themselves as Québécois—citizens of Quebec—and they saw the provincial government as their national government. Daniel Johnson had gained support with the slogan "equality or independence," echoing many Quebeckers' desire to protect their culture. The idea of creating a nationalist Canada was giving way to Quebec's separatist notions.

■ Some Quebeckers wanted the province to remain part of Canada, while others wanted to separate. The debate continues today.

Quebec and the
CONSTITUTION

Only four
provinces and
the Northwest
Territories
approved the
Charlottetown
Accord.

Robert Bourassa's Liberals won the 1970 election following Premier Daniel Johnson's unexpected death. Despite support for separation, Bourassa thought Quebec should remain part of Canada. A new separatist party called the Parti Québécois (PQ) emerged to advocate Quebec's independence from Canada. The P.Q. was led by René Lévesque. Another separatist group, the Front de Libération du Québec (FLQ), used terrorist attacks to try to achieve Quebec's sovereignty, or independence. The FLQ admitted to more than 200 bombings in the name of separation. On October 5, 1970, the FLQ's actions captured Canadians' attention during what came to be known as the October Crisis.

Four FLQ members kidnapped British Trade Commissioner James Cross. They demanded $500,000 and passage to Cuba for his return. They also wanted the FLQ **manifesto** read on national television, and the release of FLQ members convicted of bombings. Bourassa agreed to all but the release of the prisoners. Two months later, Cross was released. On October 10, FLQ members kidnapped cabinet minister Pierre Laporte. On October 17, Laporte was found dead. Within 1 month, the kidnappers were arrested and brought to trial.

After the October Crisis, separatist terrorism stopped. The government passed Bill 101 in 1977, making French Quebec's official language.

René Lévesque became the premier of Quebec in 1976. He proposed that Quebec become an independent country with an economic association to Canada. This meant Quebec would use Canadian currency, and goods would flow freely across the borders. On May 20, 1980, Quebeckers were asked to vote on the issue of separation. Sixty percent of the population voted against separation.

FURTHER UNDERSTANDING

Bill 101 The legislation that increased the use of French in workplaces, government, and courts is known as Bill 101. English-speaking schools were restricted. English Quebeckers protested Bill 101, and many businesses moved their head offices out of the province.

Front de Libération du Québec (FLQ) The FLQ was a separatist group that, in its beginnings, received support from Quebeckers. After the death of Pierre Laporte, Quebeckers lost sympathy for the group.

New Constitution When the constitution was passed, flags were lowered in Quebec, and protest marches wound through the streets of Montreal. It took 5 years for Quebec to sign the Constitution.

Parti Québécois (PQ) The Parti Québécois was the political party that challenged Bourassa in the 1970 election. The PQ won 23 percent of the popular vote and seven seats in the National Assembly. In 1976, the PQ won the provincial election with 41 percent of the vote and 71 seats.

■ Prime Minister Pierre Trudeau met with Queen Elizabeth II in 1982 to sign Canada's Constitution. Canada is governed under this constitution, which combined the previous constitutional acts and added a charter of rights and freedoms.

French–English relations suffered in 1981, when Prime Minister Trudeau met with Canada's premiers to discuss a new constitution. Lévesque was not in attendance, and the premiers reached a decision without consulting Quebec. The amendments were passed in Parliament in December. In 1982, Queen Elizabeth arrived to sign the Constitution, making Canada fully independent. Quebec did not support the legislation or attend the ceremony.

When Brian Mulroney was elected prime minister in 1984, he promised to bring the country together. In 1987, he gathered the premiers at Meech Lake, outside of Ottawa, to discuss a new constitutional agreement that would meet the approval of all provinces. The points of the Meech Lake Accord included distinct society status for Quebec. In addition, one-third of the Supreme Court judges would come from Quebec, changes to the constitution regarding powers of government would be approved by all provinces, provinces could opt out of federal programs to create their own programs with federal funding, and Quebec would control its own immigration policy. The provincial legislatures had until 1990 to pass the accord. In 1990, two provinces

rejected the deal, and the Meech Lake Accord was abandoned.

Mulroney tried again with the Charlottetown Accord in 1992, which included self-government for Native Peoples, new provincial powers, and distinct society status for Quebec. All Canadians were asked to vote on the proposal. Only four provinces and the Northwest Territories approved the accord.

Quebec still wanted to acquire status as a distinct society. A new political party, the Bloc Québécois, was created. The party, led by Lucien Bouchard, became the official opposition in the House of Commons in 1993. In 1995, Quebec held another referendum asking citizens if they wanted to separate from Canada. The results were close. Quebeckers wanted to stay in Canada, but changes would have to be made to keep them part of the country.

In 1998, the Supreme Court of Canada ruled that Quebec could not leave Canada without negotiations. Still, Quebec's place in Canada needed to be determined, and the province's unique status needed to be recognized.

■ Elijah Harper is a well-known Aboriginal politician. He believed the Meech Lake Accord ignored Native Peoples' concerns. He defeated the accord by not allowing Manitoba to vote on the accord.

WESTERN Alienation

The battle between Western farmers and the federal government continued throughout the 20th century.

Quebec was not the only Canadian region to feel alienated during the second half of the twentieth century. While Quebeckers felt separated by their language, heritage, and culture, Westerners felt they were being treated unfairly by the federal government, located in the East. Tension between the East and the West began in the 1890s over the cost of transporting goods across the country. When mineral deposits were discovered in British Columbia, U.S. developers arrived with their own railroads to remove them. To compete with the U.S. lines, the Canadian Pacific Railway (CPR) asked the federal government to help it extend its line over the Crowsnest Pass into British Columbia. Prairie farmers paid high freight charges and did not feel the CPR should be given any money. Despite the farmers' opposition, the government agreed to give the CPR $3.3 million in 1897. In exchange, the CPR agreed to reduce its rates. This new rate was known as the "Crow Rate."

Over the years, the CPR lobbied to renegotiate the Crow Rate because it did not reflect the railway's cost to transport grain. Western farmers wanted the rate to remain unchanged. A compromise was reached, and the Western Grain Transportation Act was passed in 1983. This act allowed an increase in the cost of shipping grain, but it restricted the increase to no more than 10 percent of the world price for grain. The federal government would pay shipping costs above that percentage. This created an increase in costs for farmers.

By 1995, the Crow Rate was eliminated. Many people feared that the added costs would cause a decrease in grain production for export. Others predicted that more grain would be sent to the United States rather than east to the rest of Canada. The battle between Western farmers and the federal government continued throughout the twentieth century.

In 1980, the federal government's National Energy Program (NEP) created

FURTHER UNDERSTANDING

Alienation Alienation is the separation from, and hostile feelings toward, another group of individuals. Westerners felt alienated by the Eastern provinces of Canada.

Direct democracy A direct democracy is a system in which every person votes on every issue. In a direct democracy, all citizens of a nation can vote for or against specific legislations.

■ Farming is one of western Canada's primary industries. Other industries include fishing, forestry, and mining.

even more alienation in the West. Through the NEP, the federal government attempted to gain more control over the western oil and gas industry. The NEP limited foreign investment as well as controlled pricing and profit. Alberta's Premier Peter Lougheed criticized the federal government for assuming provincial powers.

Western alienation occasionally gave rise to separatist movements. Many Western political parties have tried to bring the region's concerns to Ottawa. In the 1920s, farmers created the Progressive Party.

Representatives of this party spoke about free trade, nationalizing railways, direct democracy, and Western rights. The Social Credit party and Co-operative Commonwealth Federation (CCF) party were created when the Progressive Party dissolved in the 1930s. The CCF eventually became the New Democratic Party (NDP). Later in the twentieth century, other political parties, including the Western Canada Concept (WCC) and the Reform Party, were formed. These parties aimed to reduce western feelings of alienation.

NATIONAL ENERGY PROGRAM

In 1980, Prime Minister Pierre Trudeau announced the National Energy Program (NEP). The NEP had three aims: to increase the percentage of Canadian ownership in the oil and gas industry, to protect Canadian consumers from oil price **fluctuations** due to changes initiated by the Oil Producing Exporting Countries (OPEC), and to use some of the wealth generated by western resources for federal programs.

Under the NEP, special taxes made it difficult for foreign companies to operate in Canada's oil and gas industry. Canadian oil companies were also forced to keep their prices low for Canadian use.

Many Westerners felt the NEP unfairly took the region's wealth from the people and provinces who worked to produce the resources.

The NEP came to an end in 1984 when the Progressive Conservatives (PC) entered office. The PC government removed many petroleum related taxes and relaxed controls on the industry. Production and employment in the industry soared.

■ World oil prices quadrupled from 1973 to 1974. Oil prices increased significantly again in 1979. As a result, Pierre Trudeau's government introduced the National Energy Program to control energy resources.

IMMIGRATION
and Multiculturalism

Canada has always been one of the world's primary destinations for immigrants. After World War II, Canada experienced a surge in immigration. Nearly 1.5 million people arrived in Canada between 1945 and 1957. Many came from Germany, Great Britain, Hungary, Italy, the Netherlands, Poland, and the Ukraine. A large number of these immigrants were European refugees who no longer had homes or who could not safely return to their country of origin. Most of the newcomers settled in Canada's major cities, such as Montreal, Toronto, and Vancouver.

Over time, immigration policies have changed to restrict the migration of some groups and to make it easier for other groups to enter Canada. In 1967, ethnic and national immigration restrictions were removed. The government used a point system to evaluate possible immigrants. This system evaluated education, job skills and demand for those skills, as well as the ability to speak and write English or French. This provided opportunity for people who lived in countries that were not previously allowed to immigrate to Canada to move to this country. With further changes to the immigration policy in 1978, more restrictions were eliminated, enabling African, Chinese, Latin American, South East Asian, and West Indian people to move to Canada.

While many people immigrate to Canada, others arrive seeking refugee status. Although some of these people are actual refugees, fleeing war, persecution, or disaster, many others are seeking to escape poverty and hope to bypass the official immigration process. How to deal with

FURTHER UNDERSTANDING

Cultural mosaic The population of Canada is composed of many different cultures with separate traditions, beliefs, and customs. A group of many different cultures that all remain distinct is a cultural mosaic.

Immigration policies The Immigration Act has changed several times since World War II. These changes eliminated the preference for U.S. and European immigrants, and opened the process to people who live in many other countries. These changes to immigration policies have resulted in a more diverse culture in Canada.

Refugees Refugees are people who leave their country to live in another country. They are usually trying to escape war, persecution, or natural disasters.

■ Canadians celebrate multiculturalism through festivals. Caribana, North America's largest street festival, has been held in Toronto since 1967.

this influx of people is an issue that continues to confront Canada in the twenty-first century.

For quite some time, newcomers to Canada have been encouraged to retain their cultural heritage while adopting the ways of their new country. The cultural mosaic in Canadian society has been protected since the 1970s, when the federal government first appointed a minister for multiculturalism.

In 1971, the federal government introduced the Multiculturalism Policy to protect cultural differences while encouraging all citizens to participate in the development of Canadian society. The policy stated that all Canadians, regardless of ethnic background, should contribute to Canadian society while preserving and building their traditional cultural heritage.

The government hoped this would strengthen national unity.

In 1987, Prime Minister Brian Mulroney introduced the Multiculturalism Act. This legislation stated that the government would "recognize all Canadians as full and equal participants in Canadian society." This Act also attempted to address issues that concerned Canada's visible minorities.

Many people in Canada still have a strong connection to their cultural heritage, and the country maintains the cultural mosaic it developed decades ago. Although cultural diversity is an important feature of Canadian society and an official policy of the federal government, **discrimination** and inequality are still problems in twenty-first century Canada.

DIEFENBAKER'S UNITY

Prime Minister John Diefenbaker, unlike most other prime ministers, was not English or French. He had a German background. As a lawyer, he advocated against discrimination, which he continued after being elected prime minister.

Diefenbaker felt that national unity could only be achieved if Canadian society was based on equality and not ethnic background. He favoured a policy of "unhyphenated Canadianism." This meant citizens should consider themselves Canadian first, rather than "Russian Canadian" or "Polish Canadian."

While prime minister, Diefenbaker put his policy of equality into action. He appointed an Aboriginal senator and a Ukrainian member of Parliament. He also appointed the first woman to a cabinet posting.

His 1960 Canadian Bill of Rights recognized and guaranteed basic rights for all citizens. This legislation included the right to free speech, freedom of the press, freedom of assembly, freedom of religion, and equal treatment under the law. The Canadian Bill of Rights spurred some provinces to pass human rights acts as well. It was also the model for the Canadian Charter of Rights and Freedoms, which became law in 1982.

■ John Diefenbaker's most important contribution to Canada was the Bill of Rights. The bill enforced equality for all races and religions.

Canada's NATIVE Peoples

Early in Canada's history, Native Peoples were encouraged to abandon their traditional ways of life and become part of a society based on European culture. Treaties were signed between various Native groups and the government. These treaties dictated where Native Peoples would live. In 1876, Parliament passed the Indian Act. This act intended to protect Native Peoples' land and promote the assimilation of Native Peoples into mainstream Canadian society. Native Peoples could not leave their reserves without special passes, and their children were sent to residential schools. Some people believed the Indian Act did not conform to Canadian law and that it violated the idea of equality.

In 1969, a government White Paper, or official report, proposed that the federal government dissolve the Indian Act and Department of Indian Affairs. By eliminating the Indian Act, Native Peoples would have exactly the same rights as other Canadians.

Aboriginal groups objected to the proposal. They believed a plan to dissolve the Indian Act and Department of Indian Affairs ignored the land claims and treaty issues that had been disputed for years. They felt it would affect their lobbying efforts for Aboriginal rights in Canada. Many Native Peoples believed political activity was the only way to fight the White Paper.

The National Indian Brotherhood, which became the Assembly of First Nations in 1980, was established by Native Peoples to represent Canada's Aboriginal population. After being lobbied by this group, the government decided not to proceed with the proposal, but instead tried to grant Native Peoples control over their own affairs in the 1970s, 1980s, and 1990s.

FURTHER UNDERSTANDING

Indian Act The Indian Act is the federal legislation enacted in 1876 that dictates how Aboriginal reserves are operated and who is entitled to Native Peoples status.

Gustafsen Lake Gustafsen Lake was the site of a violent stand-off beginning when Native Peoples at the 1995 Sundance Spiritual Festival would not leave Gustafsen Lake because of unresolved land claim issues. The conflict lasted from June to September and captured the attention of the entire country.

■ Aboriginal rights advocate Phil Fontaine resigned as Chief Commissioner of the Indian Claims Commission in 2003 to run for National Chief.

In 1990, relations between Native Peoples and the government became more strained. A land dispute between town officials of Oka, Quebec, and Mohawk peoples from the Kanesatake reserve became an armed conflict, known as the Oka Stand-off. The Mohawk peoples refused to allow developers to build a golf course on sacred Mohawk land. The Mohawk peoples had taken legal action against the development, but they failed. To prevent the development, they blockaded a bridge leading to the area. Some protestors wore masks and carried weapons.

The courts ordered the Mohawk peoples to move, but they refused. On July 11, a gunshot was fired, and a policeman was killed. Within hours, about 1,000 police officers were stationed at the barricade. The barricade prevented entrance to, and exit from, the area. No food or medicine could cross into the Mohawk community.

Negotiations were stalled until August, when food and medicine were allowed into the reserve. Once supplies began moving into the Mohawk community, the government and Mohawk protestors met to discuss a **resolution**.

Negotiations between the Mohawk peoples and the government were unsuccessful. The Canadian Army replaced provincial police at the barricade. The protestors continued to talk with the army, working together to remove the bridge barricade. A barricade at the entrance to the Kanesatake reserve remained intact.

On September 26, the conflict ended. It had lasted 78 days. The Mohawk peoples were acquitted of all charges. In 1997, the government bought the disputed land so the group could expand its cemetery.

Other disputes, including the 1995 Gustafsen Lake stand-off in British Columbia, have also strained Canadian government relations with Native Peoples.

■ Canadian soldier Patrick Cloutier and Saskatchewan Native Brad Laroque met in a tense stand-off at the Kanesatake reserve in Oka, Quebec, on September 1, 1990.

TECHNOLOGY in Canada

Technology has changed the way Canadians live and work.

Canadian contributions to technology and science have led to advances in many industries. For example, many Canadian doctors have earned international recognition for their contributions to the medical field. In the 1950s, a team of Canadian doctors developed the cobalt-60 machine, which uses radiation to treat cancer. In the 1960s, the first heart transplant in Canada was performed. In the 1970s, Canadians built communications satellites and the world's first IMAX theatre. In the 1980s, a Canadian travelled to space. Canada also provided NASA with the Canadarm. Computer technology swept across the country during the 1990s. Devices created in Canada, and technology developed around the world, have changed the way Canadians live and work.

After World War II, industries focussed their attention on peacetime products, such as digital computers, jets, cellophane wrap, nylon, and electric typewriters. Products created in the 1950s and 1960s changed life in Canada. One of the most revolutionary products was the television.

Television changed Canadian families' habits. Families began spending time together watching the television rather than sitting around a table discussing their lives. Canadians' ideas about fashion, their attitudes toward politics, and their view of social situations were all affected by television programs.

Over time, television has become more influential. People originally relied on television for news and information. Today, Canadians have access to 24-hour news, weather, and sports channels, and even live coverage of the Canadian parliamentary sessions.

Another revolutionary postwar technology is the Internet. What began as a 1960's military communications network exploded into a marketing, information, and communication tool. By 1993, 15 million people were using the Internet to conduct research or chat with others surfing cyberspace. By the dawn of the twenty-first century, it was estimated that a new person logged on to the Internet every 1.6 seconds.

The spread of computers in society in the 1980s and 1990s led to a new way of doing business. As computers, Internet access, and software programs became more affordable, more Canadians began telecommuting. This allows people to work from home using their computer to send information to the office. Many major Canadian companies offer telecommuting as an option to employees.

FURTHER UNDERSTANDING

Canadarm In the 1980s, Canada developed a piece of equipment used by astronauts to retrieve satellites and other equipment in space. The Canadarm has been used on many NASA space shuttle flights.

Cyberspace Since the creation of the Internet, individuals around the world have been linked by computer networks. This is known as cyberspace.

Radiation Radiation is the emission of energy as electromagnetic waves. It is used to treat cancer patients.

■ Canadarm first travelled to space aboard U.S. *Space Shuttle Columbia* in 1981.

MARSHALL MCLUHAN

Marshall McLuhan had revolutionary theories about communication. He believed that an electronic medium was more influential than what it communicated. He said "the medium is the message," a theory that was popular in the 1960s. McLuhan thought that the medium used to record the events of an era determined that culture. He also believed that linking different modes of communication, such as computers, would produce a "global village." McLuhan taught his theories at various Canadian and American universities. He also wrote a number of books on the subject of communication. McLuhan, with his studies of the effects of technology on society, is considered to be one of the most influential communications theorists of the twentieth century.

■ McLuhan was born on July 21, 1911, in Edmonton, Alberta.

MONEY MATTERS

Technology transformed Canada into an instant society. For example, the need to enter banks during business hours to complete transactions with tellers has been eliminated by Automatic Teller Machines (ATMs). These "instant tellers" have been in use since 1971. Early machines only allowed customers to withdraw cash. Now ATM customers can also pay bills and withdraw or deposit money at any time of the day or night using a convenience card. Some ATMs even offer stamps and concert tickets, and other ATMs have stock-trading capabilities. ATMs are also convenient for travellers. Canadians travelling through other countries can access their accounts through ATMs.

A variation of ATMs can be found in movie theatres. Movie-goers no longer need to stand in line to buy tickets. Automatic machines at the entrance allow people to buy their tickets and pay for drinks and snacks with their convenience cards. Technology has made money matters easier for Canadians.

■ Forty-five percent of Canadians use ATMs for their banking transactions.

Canada and the UNITED STATES

After World War II, trade between Canada and the U.S. became more important.

Canada and the United States were allies during World War II, but by the 1960s, their relationship had declined. Prime Minister John Diefenbaker and President John F. Kennedy met in 1961. Against Kennedy's wishes, Diefenbaker chose not to provide the Canadian army with nuclear weapons. During the 1962 Cuban Missile Crisis, Kennedy relied on Diefenbaker's support. The prime minister did not put Canadian aircraft on alert until the crisis was nearly over. Diefenbaker's slow reaction to the crisis caused a rift between the two political leaders.

In 1963, Diefenbaker campaigned on an anti-United States platform. He narrowly lost the election to Lester B. Pearson, who vowed to resolve the differences between the U.S. and Canada.

Pearson opposed nuclear weapons testing, but he recognized that Canada should honour promises to its U.S. and European allies that Canada would support them in times of conflict. Still, Pearson did not always agree with U.S. leaders. Pearson and President Lyndon Johnson disagreed about how to handle events during the Vietnam War. The two leaders argued about U.S. involvement in the war. During the confrontation, Johnson grabbed Pearson by his jacket and lectured him about speaking out against U.S. policy while in the United States.

In the 1970s and 1980s, Prime Minister Pierre Trudeau attempted to reduce U.S. influence on Canadian culture. Trudeau also tried to establish foreign policy that set Canada apart from the United States. He wanted to create trading partners other than the U.S. and decrease Canada's dependence on its southern neighbour.

After World War II, trade between Canada and the U.S. became more important. Also, many U.S. companies invested money in Canadian resources. In 1974, Trudeau established the Foreign Investment Review Agency (FIRA) to

FURTHER UNDERSTANDING

Acid rain In the 1980s, acid rain became a major environmental concern. This rain was made acidic by pollutants from factories and power stations. Due to prevailing wind patterns, more than half of Canada's acid rain came from the United States.

Cuban Missile Crisis In October 1962, the United States demanded the removal of a Russian-built nuclear missile base in Cuba. The two nations remained in a stand-off for several days before Russia removed the missiles.

■ Prime Minister Pierre Trudeau and U.S. President Richard Nixon had a strained relationship. Nixon disliked Trudeau's views about socialism.

monitor U.S. and other foreign interests in Canadian businesses.

Prime Minister Brian Mulroney worked to develop a positive relationship with the United States. In 1985, he dissolved FIRA and replaced it with Investment Canada. Mulroney and President Ronald Reagan sang Irish folk songs together at talks that became known as the "Shamrock Summit." The two men met frequently and established many defence arrangements and joint ventures.

Although Mulroney saw the U.S. as an ally, he took a stand against certain issues. In the 1980s, acid rain became a serious environmental concern. Sulfuric and nitrous oxides found in the rain contaminated Canada's forests and lakes. While Canadian companies contributed to the problem, these poisons were brought to Canada largely from the United States' automobiles and industries. Mulroney asked the U.S. government to help solve the problem of acid rain, but Reagan did not act on the issue. When President George Bush was elected to office, the U.S. Congress passed legislation to control acid rain.

The economic ties between the two countries were highlighted by the building of the St. Lawrence Seaway in the 1950s. This project allowed large ocean-going freighters to bypass the rapids of the St. Lawrence River and enter the Great Lakes. In 1949, the Canadian government decided to build the seaway. In 1954, the U.S. agreed to help. Each country would finance the portion of the project that fell within its territory. The seaway was designed and built mostly by Canadians. It involved blasting rapids out of the river, flooding towns, relocating thousands of people, and rerouting transportation routes. The St. Lawrence Seaway opened in 1959, and was seen as a step toward strengthening the bond between Canada and the United States. These economic ties would be tightened in the 1990s with the North American Free Trade Agreement (NAFTA).

■ Since 1959, more than 2 billion tonnes of cargo have moved to and from Canada, the United States, and nearly 50 other countries via the St. Lawrence Seaway.

anada and the COLD WAR

Although the Cold
War did not
involve any
physical fighting,
war was a
constant threat.

After World War II, relations between the United States and the Soviet Union were tense. The Soviet Union had occupied parts of eastern Europe and established communist governments in this region. A dispute over Berlin, which was controlled by France, Great Britain, the Soviet Union, and the United States, further strained relations between the superpowers. This started the Cold War. Although the Cold War did not involve any physical fighting, war was a constant threat.

One of the first Cold War disputes centred around the rebuilding of western European countries after World War II. The U.S. wanted to help western Europe rebuild after the war. The Soviet Union wanted to prevent these nations from rebuilding. The U.S. proposed the Marshall Plan. Canada, which had already loaned a large sum of money to Britain, joined the Marshall Plan and sent another $706 million in raw materials, equipment, and food to Europe.

This plan hastened the recovery of western European countries.

Hostilities between the U.S. and the Soviet Union resulted in a war in Korea in 1950. After World War II, the United States occupied the southern half of Korea, and the Soviet Union occupied the northern half. In June 1950, North Korea sent 100,000 troops to South Korea. The U.S. asked the United Nations to help defend South Korea. The United Nations provided support. The Canadian military contributed three navy destroyers, air-transport troops, and ground troops. Of the 27,000 Canadian troops who fought in the Korean War, 300 died and 1,000 were wounded.

During the Korean War, the United States doubled the size of its air force and navy and tripled the size of its army. Canada also increased its military. In 1952, Canada spent two-fifths of the federal budget—$2 billion—on defence. At the same time, the Soviet Union developed

FURTHER UNDERSTANDING

Marshall Plan The European Recovery Program, commonly known as the Marshall Plan, was an aid program established by the U.S. to reduce the hunger, homelessness, sickness, unemployment, and political restlessness of the 270 million people in western Europe at the end of World War II. Marshall Plan money was used to feed and house individuals and rebuild Europe's devastated infrastructure. The Marshall Plan cost American taxpayers nearly $12 billion—plus $1 billion in loans—that were repaid over four years. The Marshall Plan significantly reduced the time it took western Europe to recover from the war.

■ One of Lester B. Pearson's first acts as prime minister was to meet with U.S. President John F. Kennedy. Pearson hoped to repair Canada's relationship with the United States.

an atomic bomb, and both the U.S. and the Soviet Union competed to build more powerful nuclear weapons. The Soviet Union launched a space satellite. This act displayed the nation's technological ability to launch missiles into the U.S. Both countries developed highly destructive, long-range missiles that were intended to discourage nuclear war.

The Canadian North was critical for U.S. defence against a Soviet attack. A line of radar stations, called the Distant Early Warning (DEW) Line, was set up across Alaska, Arctic Canada, and Greenland to warn of air strikes. Fighter planes in North Bay, Ontario, prepared to intercept potential Soviet bombers. As the threat of nuclear war increased, many people built bomb shelters in which they stored canned goods, clothing, blankets, and games.

Tensions mounted during the 1962 Cuban Missile Crisis. The crisis occurred when the Soviet Union placed nuclear missiles in Cuba, 145 kilometres off the Florida coast. United States President John F. Kennedy threatened to attack if the missiles were not removed. Soviet leader Nikita Khrushchev refused to remove the missiles. For five days, the world braced for World War III. The Cuban Missile Crisis ended with a compromise and without bloodshed. The crisis caused the superpowers to recognize the danger of a nuclear war.

The threats imposed by the Cold War slowly began to decrease in the late 1960s and early 1970s. Tensions relaxed in the late 1980s, when Soviet leader Mikhail Gorbachev instituted reforms with the slogans *perestroika*, which means "restructuring," and *glasnost*, which means "openness." Gorbachev's reforms finally brought an end to the Cold War.

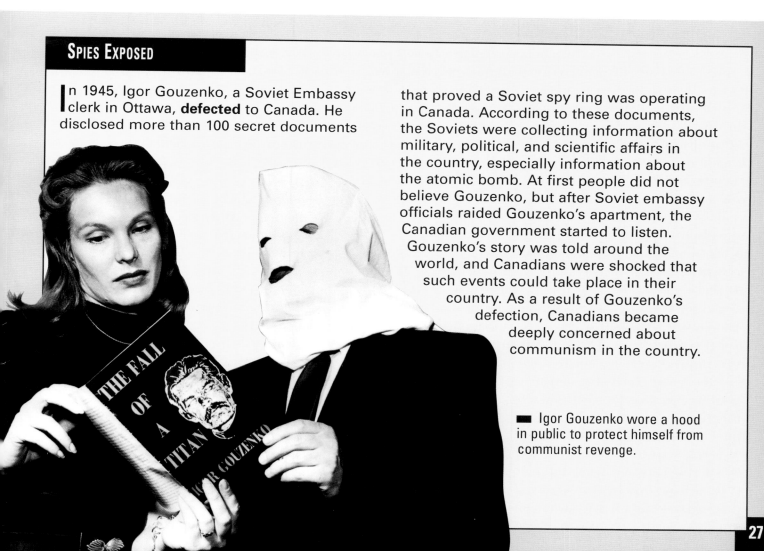

SPIES EXPOSED

In 1945, Igor Gouzenko, a Soviet Embassy clerk in Ottawa, **defected** to Canada. He disclosed more than 100 secret documents that proved a Soviet spy ring was operating in Canada. According to these documents, the Soviets were collecting information about military, political, and scientific affairs in the country, especially information about the atomic bomb. At first people did not believe Gouzenko, but after Soviet embassy officials raided Gouzenko's apartment, the Canadian government started to listen. Gouzenko's story was told around the world, and Canadians were shocked that such events could take place in their country. As a result of Gouzenko's defection, Canadians became deeply concerned about communism in the country.

■ Igor Gouzenko wore a hood in public to protect himself from communist revenge.

Canada and the UNITED NATIONS

Since World War II, Canada has played an important role in preventing war and keeping peace throughout the world. Canada, together with the United Nations (UN) and other countries, has tried to prevent small conflicts from exploding into major wars that could involve many countries. The UN's first formal peacekeeping effort was initiated by Canada's Minister for External Affairs and future prime minister, Lester B. Pearson.

In 1956, Egyptian President Gamal Abdal Nasser seized the Suez Canal from Great Britain and France. Europeans saw this as a threat to free passage through the canal. Britain and France joined with Israel to attack Egypt and reclaim the canal. Pearson suggested that the UN create an emergency force to maintain peace while an agreement was reached between the two sides. This action helped stop the fighting and resolved the Suez Crisis in a matter of days. The success of this effort prompted more peacekeeping missions around the world. Canada has taken part in every UN peacekeeping mission.

During the Korean War, Canadian peacekeepers joined the effort to keep peace in Asia. The UN ordered North Korea to withdraw from South Korea, but it refused. The UN deployed a military force to protect South Korea. This was the UN's first armed action. The troops consisted of soldiers from around the world, including Australia, Canada, Great Britain, South Africa, Turkey, and the U.S.

While in Korea, Canadian forces insisted that they participate as part of the UN forces and not the U.S. forces occupying South Korea. For about 3 years, approximately 27,000 soldiers from the Royal Canadian Navy, Royal Canadian Army, and Royal Canadian Air Force served in Korea. When the Korean War ended, Canada participated in the United Nations Command Military Armistice Commission. This commission settled disagreements and violations of the 1953 Armistice Agreement. Canada remains a member of this commission.

FURTHER UNDERSTANDING

Ceasefires Orders to stop fighting are called cease-fires.

Coalition The formation of a union between different groups is a coalition.

Deployed Military personnel who have been called into action have been deployed.

Liaison A liaison, like the United Nations, opens the lines of communication and co-operation between different units of an organization.

■ The Royal Canadian Regiment fought as part of the Commonwealth Division during the Korean War.

Middle East

The United Nations Truce Supervision Organization, established in 1948, maintains cease-fires. Canada has participated in many Middle East missions as liaison officers, military observers, and headquarter staff for these missions.

In 1953, UN peacekeepers were sent to the Middle East, where fighting had occurred for decades. Israel wanted to keep the areas it had occupied during war and protect itself from Arab attacks. The Arabs refused to recognize the state of Israel and planned to destroy it.

After the Cold War ended, the UN began sending troops to areas before cease-fires were negotiated. This put peacekeepers at greater risk.

The Persian Gulf War in 1990 was the first large-scale crisis after the Cold War. Iraq invaded Kuwait. A UN-sponsored coalition force used advanced military technology and air campaigns against Iraq. About 4,000 Canadian soldiers took part in the Gulf War.

The United Nations Iraq-Kuwait Observer Mission was created in 1991. Five Canadian military observers work with this mission. Canadians have also participated in the United Nations Special Commission, which was created to inspect and, if necessary, destroy biological, chemical, and nuclear weapons.

Cyprus

One of Canada's longest peacekeeping missions took place in Cyprus. Fighting between Greek and Turkish populations occurred in Cyprus in 1963. Peacekeepers from Canada, Denmark, Finland, Ireland, and Sweden arrived in Cyprus in 1964.

In 1974, Turkey invaded Cyprus. The UN sent more troops to Cyprus. To stop the fighting, Cyprus was divided. The north would remain under Turkish control, and the south would remain under Greek control. United Nations soldiers remained in Cyprus until 1993. A small number of Canadian soldiers remained in the country as observers.

■ There were no Canadian peacekeeper casualties during the Gulf War.

29

Canada as PEACEKEEPER

The actions of some Canadian soldiers in Somalia tarnished the reputation of Canadian peacekeepers.

Africa

Canada has taken part in many United Nations missions in Africa, including one in Somalia. Civil war, drought, and famine devastated Somalia. In November 1991, battles broke out between warring clans. The food supply was used as a tool to gain support. Those who supported the clans ate, and those who did not support the clans starved.

The UN negotiated a cease-fire. The UN also tried to help more than 1 million starving Somalis. Armed gangs had hijacked food and supplies sent by other countries. Canada became part of the UN coalition force sent to protect the food distribution system. The actions of a few members of the Canadian Airborne Regiment involved in this effort tarnished Canada's reputation as the one of the world's most reliable peacekeepers.

Rwanda

In 1993, UN peacekeepers arrived in Rwanda to help monitor a cease-fire between the Hutu government and the Tutsi opposition. Canada provided two of the three senior officers in command of the UN force.

When the presidents of Rwanda and Burundi were killed in a plane crash, violence erupted. Soon, UN soldiers were being attacked and killed. Many western governments withdrew their soldiers from Rwanda, reducing the number of troops from 2,548 to 270.

By 1994, a new government had been established, and the war had ended. More than 500,000 people had died. Four million others had fled the country or were left homeless. Twenty-seven UN workers died. Trials against those responsible for violations, such as genocide, began in 1997.

FURTHER UNDERSTANDING

Famine Countries that suffer from an extreme scarcity of food are experiencing a famine.

Genocide Genocide is the intentional extermination of a race of people.

Sanctions Sanctions are actions taken to punish a country that is violating a law or code of practice. Some sanctions are introduced to change, rather than punish, such practice.

War crimes Crimes that violate the international laws of war are known as war crimes.

■ Since 1954, Canada has had much contact with the Middle East through peacekeeping missions. Canada has taken part in every peacekeeping mission in the Middle East.

The Balkans

In 1991, Slovenia and Croatia declared independence from Yugoslavia. Bosnia-Herzegovina followed in 1992. The Yugoslavian army went to war to protect Serbians living in these areas. The fighting led to an international refugee crisis, leaving approximately 1.7 million people homeless in the former Yugoslavia.

Canadians participated in the European Community Monitor Mission from September 1991 to August 1994. This mission, which was not part of the UN, monitored and reported on the elements of cease-fire agreements and helped people caught in the fighting.

In 1992, the United Nations Protection Force was established to create peace and security in the region. The UN imposed sanctions against Yugoslavia, such as a "no-fly" zone to prevent the Serbian air force from helping the Bosnian Serbs. Canadian Forces personnel were assigned to the North Atlantic Treaty Organization (NATO) aircraft monitoring this zone. Canada transported more than 10,000 passengers and 23,148 tons of relief

supplies into the country. As well, Major General Lewis MacKenzie led a UN peacekeeping force in Bosnia, which included about 1,000 Canadian soldiers.

In addition to peacekeeping duties, Canada sent a War Crimes Investigation Team to help the United Nations Commission of Experts gather evidence of war crimes and rights violations during the conflict. Peace agreements were signed in 1997 and 1999, but the former Yugoslavia could still erupt into violence.

SCANDAL IN SOMALIA

The actions of some Canadian soldiers in Somalia tarnished the reputation of Canadian peacekeepers. About 900 members of the Canadian Airborne Regiment arrived in Somalia in 1992. Soldiers on patrol shot two Somalis on March 4, 1993—one was wounded, and the other died. Twelve days later, a teenaged Somali was tortured and killed on the base. A Canadian soldier took photographs of the torturous acts. These images, along with videotape of the conduct of these soldiers, became public. The regiment was disbanded, and its actions were investigated. Many officers lost their jobs, and some soldiers were tried and sent to prison for their actions.

■ The Canadian peacekeeping program began in 1947, and is still active today. Canadian peacekeepers travel to countries around the world, such as Egypt, India, and Iraq, to monitor the use of biological weapons, maintain cease-fires, and ensure the safe transport of relief supplies to victims of war-torn countries.

FOREIGN Policy Since 1945

1945 Canada joins the United Nations to help prevent another world war.

1948 The United Nations Truce Supervision Organization, established in 1948, maintains cease-fires.

1949 Canada joins the North Atlantic Treaty Organization (NATO).

1956 Lester B. Pearson helps solve the Suez Canal Crisis. One year later, he wins the Nobel Peace Prize.

1962 Prime Minister John Diefenbaker and U.S. President John F. Kennedy disagree about the action needed to end the Cuban Missile Crisis.

1963 Prime Minister John Diefenbaker campaigns on an anti-U.S. platform.

1964 Prime Minister Pearson meets with French President Charles de Gaulle to improve economic and cultural relations between the two countries.

1973 Prime Minister Trudeau's visit to China to discuss trade partnerships meets with controversy because China is a communist country.

1975 Prime Minister Trudeau establishes the Foreign Investment Review Agency (FIRA) to monitor U.S. and other foreign interests in Canadian businesses.

■ In October 1973, Pierre Trudeau became the first Canadian prime minister to make an official visit to China.

1982 Prime Minister Trudeau establishes a new Canadian Constitution, making Canada independent of Great Britain. Queen Elizabeth arrives to participate in the ceremony.

1985 Prime Minister Mulroney replaces the Foreign Investment Review Agency with the less restrictive Investment Canada.

1991 Canada joins UN-sponsored coalition forces involved in the Persian Gulf War.

1993 Canada signs a trade agreement with the U.S. and Mexico to form the North American Free Trade Agreement (NAFTA).

1998 Prime Minister Chrétien becomes the first Canadian prime minister in 22 years to meet with Cuban President Fidel Castro.

2001 Canada sends troops to Afghanistan in response to terrorist attacks on the World Trade Center in New York.

CANADIAN INTERNATIONAL DEVELOPMENT AGENCY (CIDA)

- CIDA was formed in 1968 to handle Canada's foreign aid.
- Much of Canada's foreign policy is in the form of aid to other countries.
- In 1994 and 1995, Canada spent $2.5 billion on foreign assistance, including donations to specific countries, UN organizations, and nongovernmental organizations in more than 100 countries.
- The International Development Research Centre, established in 1970, finances research into changing science and technology so it can be used by countries in the developing world.

■ Canada's international foreign aid brings people together to pursue a common goal. Countries around the world, such as Ghana, benefit from these programs.

INDUSTRY in Canada

The prosperity of the 1950s and 1960s was challenged in the early 1970s.

Once World War II ended, Canadians returned to their regular routines. The recession many feared would follow the war did not occur. Instead, Canada's economy boomed. Canadian industries flourished. Large oil deposits were discovered in Alberta in 1947, bringing both wealth and new resource development to the province. In the 1950s, the government built a trans-Canada pipeline to transport Alberta's oil east and west. Copper, zinc, and uranium mines discovered in Saskatchewan further fueled the Western economy. British Columbia and Manitoba built hydroelectric plants. Atlantic Canada was thriving, too. Military bases set up along the east coast during the war provided jobs for many Canadians. Ontario and Quebec continued to employ thousands of people in factories and other businesses. Postwar prosperity was experienced from coast to coast.

After years of war rations, Canadians were eager to spend their money. The 1950s offered countless inventions and products for Canadians to buy. They purchased everything from ballpoint pens and electric can openers to new cars and homes with two-car garages. Home construction and car manufacturing were two of the country's most significant industries. However, purchasing a television set was a priority for many families.

Television affected the way products were sold in Canada. Companies began spending large sums of money on advertising to persuade Canadians to buy their products. Marketing professionals showed their products compared to the rival's product, often referred to as "Brand X" in commercials. Canadian consumers were bombarded with brand name advertisements in their newspapers, on the radio, and on television. The importance of advertising grew through the 1950s, and consumer sales grew along with it.

FURTHER UNDERSTANDING

Advertising In the 1950s, advertising became an effective tool to promote a product. Companies began using television and radio ads in an effort to persuade consumers to buy a product.

Embargo An embargo is an official suspension of commerce.

Recession Following World War II, it was thought there would be a temporary drop in economic prosperity. Instead, an increase in industry and technology paved the way for economic stability.

Energy Crisis In 1973, oil prices increased as a result of decreased oil exports. As a result of the steep increase in the cost of oil, inflation reached more than 10 percent in 1974–1975, and unemployment increased to more than 7 percent in 1975. The National Energy Program (NEP) was developed to gain control of energy resources.

■ The cable television industry was established in Canada in the 1950s. Today, there are more than 30 Canadian cable programming services.

During the 1950s, organized labour increased, and so did the power of unions. More than 30 percent of Canadian workers were members of a union in the 1950s.

As industry and manufacturing skyrocketed, so did the population. Immigration and the baby boom boosted Canada's population. From 1946 to 1961, the country's population increased from 12 million to 18 million. Most of these people lived in cities and worked in the booming industrial sector.

The prosperity of the 1950s and 1960s was challenged in the early 1970s. The Energy Crisis, which lasted from October 1973 until March 1974, worried many people. There was an international oil embargo by the Arab members of the Organization of Petroleum Exporting Countries (OPEC). These countries protested U.S. military support of Israel in the 1973 Middle East War. Without foreign oil, Canadians were concerned about how they would meet their energy needs.

In 1979, world oil prices increased 150 percent, causing a global recession. Oil companies had to pass the extra costs on to consumers. This created inflation, a downturn in the economy, and higher unemployment in western countries. The U.S. purchased oil from Canada. When Canada raised its oil prices to stay competitive, the U.S. became concerned. Conflict also arose in Canada.

Debates raged over the price of oil within Canada and who should receive the profits from oil sales outside of Canada. Alberta was Canada's major oil producer. Alberta politicians argued that the petroleum resources belonged to the province, and it should be able to sell gas and oil at a competitive price. This meant increased oil prices in Canada. The provincial and federal governments continued to debate the energy issue after the National Energy Policy was put in place in 1980.

■ The National Energy Program was dismantled by the Progressive Conservative government after it was elected to the House of Commons in 1984.

The Canadian ECONOMY

By the end of the 1970s, the federal government was spending $500 million per year on regional development to boost the economy. At the same time, inflation was high, and the cost of providing social and economic services was climbing. The federal debt was also growing quickly. Prime Minister Pierre Trudeau argued that the only way to cut the deficit was to cut government spending. Given the high unemployment rate, few people were willing to see child benefit payments, pension payments, and unemployment payments reduced.

In 1979, Prime Minister Joe Clark added a gasoline tax to the budget. Clark hoped the gas tax would reduce gasoline consumption and ensure that Canada became self-sufficient in oil products by 1990. Revenue from the gas tax would also be used to reduce the deficit. This displeased Canadians and led to a vote of non-confidence and a Liberal return to office in 1980.

In the 1980s, the economic recession worsened, and the federal deficit continued to increase. Complicating the issue, thousands of Canadian workers were unemployed. The unemployment rate reached 12.9 percent in 1982. This was higher than it had been in the Great Depression of the 1930s.

The value of the Canadian dollar dropped internationally to only 70.2 cents U.S. The dollar continued to drop 1 to 2 cents per year. In 1991, the Canadian dollar recovered and was worth 83 cents U.S. The recovery did not last. In 1999, it took $1.52 Canadian to buy $1 U.S. By 2001, $1 Canadian was worth 63 cents U.S.

The slow economic trend continued in the 1990s. Inflation and interest rates remained high, and the worst recession since the Great Depression swept the country in the early part of the decade. At the same time, unemployment took a new twist. Thousands of Canadians

FURTHER UNDERSTANDING

Deficit A deficit is the amount of money a government spends above what it receives in taxes and other revenue.

National debt The total amount of money owed by a government to pay off loans is the national debt. In 1944, Canada's debt was $8 billion. It increased to $19 billion by 1974, $91 billion by 1981, and $458 billion by 1993.

Stagflation Stagflation is a combination of high inflation and increased unemployment.

■ At 39 years of age, Joe Clark became Canada's youngest prime minister when he was elected in 1979.

became victims of a new economic **phenomenon**—downsizing. Like many U.S. companies, Canadian corporations began to reduce staff in order to remain competitive in the global marketplace. Businesses merged, and excess employees were laid off due to budget restrictions. Downsizing continued as the country moved into the twenty-first century.

There was a gradual recovery in the marketplace in the mid-1990s. The Canadian economy performed well, and many Canadians finally found work. Unemployment rates began to drop, and incomes increased. Productivity also began to grow as inflation decreased. By 1995, the unemployment rate dipped below 10 percent and hovered around 7.9 percent in 1998.

After a period of stagflation, the federal government concentrated on reducing the deficit. Even as the government began reducing the deficit, the national debt remained large and served as a reminder of the recession. The last time the debt decreased was during the year 1969 to 1970. At that time, the debt dropped from $19.4 billion to $19.2 billion. By comparison, between 1993 and 1997, the debt increased by more than $73 billion. By 2000, Canada's national debt was $576.8 billion, and it cost taxpayers $42 billion per year in interest payments. While the economy had picked up significantly in the late 1990s, Canadians entered the twenty-first century with guarded optimism about their economic future.

■ Canada's unemployment rate was 7.8 percent in May 2003.

The Start of FREE TRADE

The North American Free Trade Agreement created the second largest free trade area in the world.

In 1989, Prime Minister Brian Mulroney and President George Bush put the Canada–United States Free Trade Agreement (FTA) into effect. This agreement called for the eventual elimination of tariffs and the reduction of other trade barriers between the two countries. By 1998, most tariffs, or charges applied to imported and exported goods, had been eliminated. The FTA was changed and expanded to become the North American Free Trade Agreement (NAFTA) in 1994.

NAFTA also called for the eventual removal of tariffs on most goods sold and produced in North America. While the FTA was set up to reduce or eliminate tariffs between Canada and the U.S., NAFTA expanded its scope to include Mexico in the agreement. NAFTA called for the elimination of tariffs on half of all goods shipped from the U.S. to Mexico. The leaders also agreed that by 2003, almost all tariffs on goods produced in Canada and Mexico would be eliminated. Other tariffs would be removed gradually over the next 14 years. The specifications of the FTA would remain in place.

NAFTA removed restrictions in many categories, including automobiles and auto parts, computers, and agriculture. Investment barriers between the countries were lifted as well, and the political leaders hoped the agreement would encourage investment across the borders. Such issues as minimum wage, working conditions, and environmental responsibility were later added to the agreement.

FURTHER UNDERSTANDING

North American Free Trade Agreement (NAFTA) Many people believe that Canadian producers are more successful because of NAFTA. For example, because of NAFTA, Canadian producers have a larger buying public. Consumers are also benefiting from this agreement as more competition drives prices down and increases service and quality. The Canadian economy has grown due to NAFTA. Trade and investment between the three countries have soared, with total goods traded across the continent valued at more than $752 billion in 1998. About $1.5 billion in services and goods cross the Canada–U.S. border every day.

■ Mexico's economy declined significantly in 1995. This had a negative impact on the standard of living for most Mexicans and led to an increase in extreme poverty. Since then, the economy has been recovering.

In 1992, Prime Minister Brian Mulroney, Mexican President Carlos Salinas de Gortari, and U.S. President George Bush signed NAFTA. It was not until 1993 that the legislatures of these three countries would approve the agreement. In the United States, NAFTA split each of the political parties. Labour and environmental groups rallied against the agreement. People feared production plants would be moved to Mexico, where they could find a cheaper work force and less strict environmental laws. This meant U.S. and Canadian citizens might lose their jobs and that pollution and product safety concerns would be harder to enforce. To address these concerns, the three countries presented supplemental agreements in 1993. NAFTA was narrowly approved and became official in all three countries on January 1, 1994. NAFTA created a market of 365 million consumers and the second largest free trade area in the world.

In 1994, NAFTA members began discussing the possibility of adding all Latin American countries except Cuba to the agreement.

EARLY FREE TRADE AGREEMENTS

After World War II, many countries attempted to adopt policies of free trade and fewer barriers. In 1948, the General Agreement on Tariffs and Trade (GATT) was established. This international agreement and trade organization tried to decrease or eliminate tariffs and other barriers to trade between countries. GATT insisted that each member treat all other members as they would treat their most important trade nation. If a member nation reduced a tariff for one country, all other members would enjoy the same lowered rate. If the low rate caused serious harm to the country's economy, it could withdraw that reduction.

GATT was signed by 23 countries, including Canada and the U.S., and it has resulted in reduced tariffs on thousands of items since it was created. GATT membership continued to rise until 1995, when GATT's activities were

■ In 1965, the Automotive Products Agreement was signed by (left–right) Paul Martin, Prime Minister Lester Pearson, U.S. President Lyndon Johnson, and Dean Rusk. Under the agreement, automotive products can be imported duty-free between Canada and the U.S.

taken over by the World Trade Organization (WTO).

The WTO also tries to establish international free trade. It administers trade laws and helps member countries settle trade disputes. It is stronger than GATT because it can impose trade sanctions against a country that will not remove an offending law or practice. By 2001, 142 countries were members of the WTO.

GLOBALISM

Canada has embraced the globalization of the economy and has been a willing participant in the free market that resulted from it.

In the 1960s, globalism was an idea that made Canadians think about international issues. For example, Marshall McLuhan, one of the most influential communications theorists in the twentieth century, predicted that modern communications would create a global village. By the 1990s, it was becoming apparent that he was right.

Globalism suggests that something that was once local has now become global. Globalism is often seen as a shared ownership of the world's economic resources and assets. Responsibility and control over this ownership is shifting from nations to international groups.

The world economy consists of independent countries that trade with each other in a way that benefits both parties. It is becoming a united world economy that is trading within itself.

The World Trade Organization (WTO), the International Monetary Fund, and the World Bank are examples of how power passes from the national to the global level. The development of more multinational trade agreements is a result of a turn toward globalism. Canada's involvement in NAFTA encourages the global view. Companies in Toronto can do business with companies in Mexico City or Houston nearly as easily as they can with other Canadian companies. Just as Marshall McLuhan thought, the world's borders are disappearing in many areas.

Canada embraced the globalization of the economy and was a willing participant in the free market that resulted from it. However, globalism is not restricted to trade issues. The global village can be seen in the entertainment and information industries as well. Billions of people

FURTHER UNDERSTANDING

International Monetary Fund (IMF) The IMF was established in 1945 to promote economic development and increase employment.

World Bank
The World Bank was formed by the United Nations in 1944. It offers loans to governments for purposes of reconstruction and economic development.

World Trade Organization (WTO) The WTO was created when the members of the General Agreement on Tariffs and Trade (GATT) signed a new trade pact. The WTO promotes and regulates trade between countries. It began operating on January 1, 1995.

■ In Cambodia, thousands of young women work long hours in garment factories for little pay. The World Bank and IMF promote the economic development and improve working conditions in struggling countries, such as Cambodia.

can watch a sporting event or a concert by turning on their television set. It does not matter how far away viewers are from the action—television brings them to the front row. E-mail messages and faxes are delivered to destinations across the world immediately, bringing together people from one end of the globe to the other. With globalization, borders and distance became less serious considerations.

Globalization has also increased Canada's interest in preserving the environment. Issues, such as disappearing forests and air and water pollution, have concerned Canadians since the 1960s. These problems became more important in the 1990s. People began to realize the consequences of ignoring environmental problems. For example, everyone on Earth is put at risk by the ultraviolet radiation passing through holes in the ozone layer, regardless of the location of these holes. Environmental violations in other continents and countries affect Canadians. Consequently, people have been encouraged to consider the good of the world and its survival by reducing or eliminating pollution and addressing other local environmental problems.

GLOBALIZATION AND INTERNATIONAL TRADE AGREEMENTS

International trade agreements are an integral part of globalization. However, free trade agreements such as NAFTA have caused some changes in the way business is conducted around the world. For example, California wanted to stop using MTBE, a toxic, highly water-soluble gasoline additive, because gasoline containing this material leaked into the groundwater in Santa Monica. Methanex, a Canadian manufacturer of the gasoline additive MTBE, argued that the product was safe and that a California boycott of MTBE would destroy the market.

Methanex filed a claim with a NAFTA tribunal on the grounds that California's plan to ban MTBE violates the free trade agreement. NAFTA does not discourage states and municipalities from enacting environmental regulations that are more strict than national or international standards. Instead, it provides for payment to be made to companies that are harmed by these regulations. Methanex asked for $970 million in compensation.

Other companies are arguing cases before NAFTA tribunals. The United Parcel Service in the U.S. argued that the publicly supported postal system in Canada poses unfair competition, which goes against Canada's NAFTA responsibilities.

Both of these claims, along with others, were filed under the clause that protects investments between Canada, Mexico, and the U.S. Sometimes globalism can cause new and complicated challenges for the world's nations and how they conduct business.

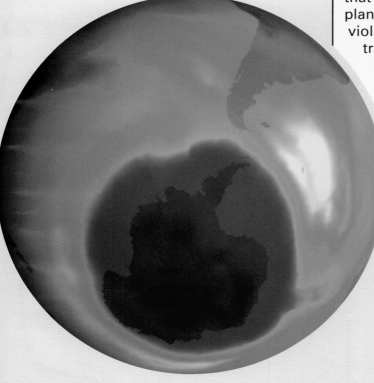

■ The ozone layer blocks most of the Sun's harmful rays. In 1985, a hole was discovered in the ozone layer over the Antarctic.

SUMMARY of Canadian History

1945 World War II comes to an end. Canada joins the United Nations.

1949 Newfoundland becomes a Canadian province.

1959 The St. Lawrence Seaway opens.

1960 The Canadian Bill of Rights is introduced by Prime Minister John Diefenbaker's government.

1965 The Maple Leaf becomes the official symbol on Canada's flag.

1970 The October Crisis begins when the FLQ kidnap British trade commissioner James Cross.

1977 Quebec passes language laws restricting the use of English.

1980 The Nation Energy Program is introduced.

1982 A new constitution is signed.

1985 Changes are made to the Indian Act.

1987 The Meech Lake Accord, which was intended to promote national unity, is not ratified.

1990 The Oka Stand-off in Quebec ends with a compromise between the Mohawk Peoples and the federal government.

1992 Like the Meech Lake Accord, the Charlottetown Accord, which was intended to promote national unity, is not successful.

1995 Quebec conducts a referendum on separation. Quebec citizens vote not to separate from Canada.

1999 The map of Canada is redrawn to include a new territory, Nunavut.

1999 The Federal government grants the U.S. a 10-year extension on the agreement to use Nanoose Bay, British Columbia, as a weapons testing site.

2000 Seventy percent of married women are employed outside the home.

■ By 2000, about 13 million Canadians over the age of 15 used the Internet at home or work.

QUIZ (answers on page 47)

Multiple Choice

Choose the best answer in the multiple choice questions that follow.

1 Why did Quebec want to separate from Canada?

a) it had an oil dispute with the federal government

b) it wanted to preserve its French language and culture

c) it did not like using Canadian dollars

2 What does it mean to have a cultural mosaic?

a) that different cultures combine to form a new, universal culture

b) a country sets up pockets of different cultures

c) newcomers maintain their traditions and cultures while becoming part of the new country

3 What did U.S. President Kennedy and Prime Minister Diefenbaker disagree about?

a) Canadian resistance to supporting the American position on the Cuban Missile Crisis

b) trade barriers

c) the price of Canadian oil and gas

4 What happened to the Canadian economy after World War II?

a) it fell into a recession, just as it had after World War I

b) it remained at pre-war levels

c) it enjoyed great prosperity

5 Why were some people worried about signing NAFTA?

a) it might cause a civil war

b) it might cause the loss of U.S. and Canadian jobs

c) it might make other countries jealous

6 What happened at Nanoose Bay?

a) Native Peoples staged a stand-off

b) weapons were tested

c) U.S. President Reagan and Prime Minister Mulroney held a summit

7 What is the October Crisis?

a) it occurred when the FLQ kidnapped British Trade Commissioner James Cross

b) it marked a drastic drop in wheat prices

c) it was a document expressing concerns about the budget

8 Which provinces accepted the National Energy Program?

a) it was accepted by all provinces

b) it was opposed by Ontario because it favoured the West

c) it was opposed by the West because it limited the region's profits and control over oil and gas

9 What was Canada's policy on immigration?

a) to allow a few immigrants into the country

b) to be one of the world's primary destinations for immigrants

c) to encourage immigration from all countries

10 What motivated the Oka Stand-off?

a) a proposed golf course on land sacred to the Mohawk Peoples

b) a treaty dispute over fishing rights

c) funding for Aboriginal reservations

Mix and Match

Match the terms in column B with the correct description in column A. There are more terms than descriptions.

A

1. Defence alliance created in 1949
2. Discovery of oil in the West
3. Introduced in 1971 to protect cultural differences
4. Passed the Official Languages Act in 1969
5. Number of married women employed outside the home in 1971
6. Leader of the Bloc Québécois
7. Won the Nobel Peace Prize in 1957

B

a) Lester B. Pearson
b) 30 percent
c) John Diefenbaker
d) Canadarm
e) North Atlantic Treaty Organization (NATO)
f) Multiculturalism Policy
g) Pierre Trudeau
h) Lucien Bouchard
i) 1940s

Time Line

Find the appropriate spot on the time line for each event listed below.

A John Diefenbaker introduces the Bill of Rights

B Brian Mulroney organizes the Meech Lake Accord

C Canada's population increases by 50 percent

D Lester B. Pearson helps resolve the Suez Canal Crisis

E Nanoose Bay is still being used as a weapons testing site

F Pierre Trudeau calls the War Measures Act into effect to protect Canadians

1930s Canada experiences the Great Depression	**1965** The maple leaf is used as the symbol on a distinctly Canadian flag	**1982** Pierre Trudeau introduces the Constitution Act and the Charter of Rights and Freedoms
1941–1961 **1**	**1969** French and English become the official languages of Canada	
1945 Canada joins the United Nations		**1987** **5**
1949 Canada joins the North Atlantic Treaty Organization	**1970** **4**	**1999** **6**
1956 **2**	**1971** More than 30 percent of married women are employed outside the home	**2000** The number of married women who are employed outside the home reaches 70 percent
1957 Lester B. Pearson wins the Nobel Peace Prize		
1960 **3**	**1974** French becomes Quebec's official language	

Conclusion

After World War II, Canada enjoyed great prosperity. The economy was strong, and unemployment was low. As a result of these favourable economic conditions, Canada's population grew by 50 percent between 1941 and 1961.

During World War II, Canada had proven itself to be independent of Great Britain and became known as a middle power. Canada had influence, but it was still too small to dominate international affairs. However, its location made it ideal for both the Atlantic and Pacific trade areas.

Following World War II, industries grew, and oil was discovered in the West, which added to the economic boom. As a result of this prosperity, social welfare programs were introduced to improve the life of Canadians.

Although Canada had a booming economy during the 1940s and 1950s, the 1960s and 1970s saw the rise of discontent. Women began lobbying for political and social equality. Aboriginal groups fought for the right to self-government and land claims. Peace protests and demonstrations were held against the deployment of nuclear weapons in Canada and weapons testing. Quebec tried to gain independence from the rest of Canada, and the West argued with the federal government about who should control the riches generated by oil and other natural resources.

Canada has enjoyed both prosperity and recession since World War II. Although it has endured many internal struggles, Canada has taken its place in the global village, and it has worked to build a more stable future.

Further Information

Suggested Reading

Brownsey, K. and Howlett, M. *The Provincial State in Canada: Politics in the Provinces and Territories.* Peterborough, ON: Broadview Press, 2001.

Cook, S. A., L. R. McLean, and K. O'Rourke. *Framing Our Past: Canadian Women's History in the Twentieth Century.* Montreal: McGill-Queen's University Press, 2001.

Lotz, J. *A Century of Service: Canada's Armed Forces from the Boer War to East Timor.* Halifax: Nova Scotia International Tattoo Society, 2000.

Mallory, Enid L. *The Remarkable Years: Canadians Remember the 20th Century.* Markham, ON: Fitzhenry & Whiteside, 2001.

Internet Resources

Canada: A People's History Online
history.cbc.ca
The online companion to CBC's award-winning television series on the history of Canada, as told through the eyes of its people. This multi-media Web site features behind-the-scenes information, games and puzzles, and discussion boards. Available in French and English.

The Canadian Encyclopedia Online
www.thecanadianencyclopedia.com
A reference for all things Canadian. In-depth history articles are accompanied by photographs, paintings, and maps. Articles can be read in both French and English.

Glossary

activism: acting in a way that supports a specific cause, often political

amendments: changes made to a law

capitalist system: an economic system in which the production and distribution of wealth is controlled mainly by individuals and corporations

communist system: a system where all possessions are owned equally

constitution: a written document that forms the set of political principles by which a country is governed

culture: the general customs and beliefs of a group of people at a specific time

defected: abanded loyalty to one's own country and moved to another country

democracy: a government that is elected by the people and has an opposition

discrimination: unfair treatment of a person or group on the basis of prejudice

fluctuations: changes or variances

immigration: the act of moving to and settling in a different country

incentives: items that encourage a person or group to complete a task or a project

inflation: a rise in prices and a drop in the value of money

legislation: a law or set of laws suggested by a government and made official by a parliament

lobbying: campaigning to influence decisions

mandatory: something that must be done or is demanded by law

manifesto: a declaration of policy, usually made by a political party

phenomenon: a remarkable development

prosperity: economic well-being

resolution: a solution to a problem

separatist: a person who believes that Quebec should be an independent country

warheads: explosive heads of missiles, torpedoes, or similar weapons

Answers

Multiple Choice	Mix and Match	Time Line
1. b)	1. e)	1. c)
2. c)	2. i)	2. d)
3. a)	3. f)	3. a)
4. c)	4. g)	4. f)
5. b)	5. b)	5. b)
6. b)	6. h)	6. e)
7. a)	7. a)	
8. c)		
9. b)		
10. a)		

Index